My First Riddle 2021

Amazing Verses

Edited By Byron Tobolik

First published in Great Britain in 2021 by:

☙Young Writers®
Est. 1991

Young Writers
Remus House
Coltsfoot Drive
Peterborough
PE2 9BF
Telephone: 01733 890066
Website: www.youngwriters.co.uk

All Rights Reserved
Book Design by Ashley Janson
© Copyright Contributors 2021
Softback ISBN 978-1-80015-510-7

Printed and bound in the UK by BookPrintingUK
Website: www.bookprintinguk.com
YB0477A

FOREWORD

Dear Reader,

Are you ready to get your thinking caps on to puzzle your way through this wonderful collection?

Young Writers are proud to introduce our new poetry competition, *My First Riddle*, designed to introduce reception pupils to the delights of poetry. Riddles are a great way to introduce children to the use of poetic expression, including description, similes and expanded noun phrases, as well as encouraging them to 'think outside the box' by providing clues without giving the answer away immediately. Some pupils were given a series of riddle templates to choose from, giving them a framework within which to shape their ideas.

Their answers could be whatever or whoever their imaginations desired; from people to places, animals to objects, food to seasons. All of us here at Young Writers believe in the importance of inspiring young children to produce creative writing, including poetry, and we feel that seeing their own riddles in print will ignite that spark of creativity.

We hope you enjoy riddling your way through this book as much as we enjoyed reading every poem we received.

CONTENTS

Arksey Primary School, Arksey

Catherine Dusi (4)	1
Martha Rushbrooke (5)	2
Lucca White (5)	3
Oliver Gale (5)	4
Edie Rollinson (5)	5
Harper Crundell (5)	6
Teodor Atkin (5)	7
Pippa Jones (5)	8
Isaac Lawrence (5)	9
Joseph Carroll (5)	10
Daisy Taylor (4)	11
Jessica Ellis (5)	12
Amelia Mangham (5)	13
Destiny Hockaday (5)	14
Jonathan Horberry	15
Brooke-Lilly Ackland (5)	16

Bright Futures School, Lymm

Joshua Thomson-Borg (11)	17
Daphne Blake (Georgia) (6)	18
Joshua Daniel Pierce (8)	19
Ayrton Ankrah (6)	20
Archie Barrow (10)	21

Gawsworth Primary School, Gawsworth

Freddie Petrie (4)	22
Reuben Cairns (5)	23
Amelie Carrier (5)	24
Hector Stallard (5)	25
Alannah Corr (5)	26
Sam Boyle (5)	27

Oscar Smith (5)	28

Grove CE Primary School, Grove

Hermione Woodley (4)	29
Bobby Saunders (5)	30
Maya Waring (5)	31
Brinley Bettson (5)	32
Darcey Austin (5)	33
George Morgan (5)	34
Flynn Bolton (4)	35
Henry Addison (5)	36
Verity Appleton (5)	37
Evie Pryce (5)	38
Victoria Jones (5)	39
George L. J. Vaughan (5)	40
Forest Slaymaker (5)	41
Noah Arthur Alencar-Martins (5)	42
James Whyte (4)	43
Jacob Penn (5)	44

Lapage Primary School, Bradford

Halimah Sadia Shaffiq (4)	45
Hamda Sabir (5)	46
Hanna Butt	47
Yahya Kalam (5)	48
Amani (5)	49
Aaila (5)	50
Haseeb Mahmood (5)	51
Dua Khan (5)	52
Kiswa Noor (5)	53
Khawlah Ayaz	54
Ajwa Nur (5)	55

Martin Wilson School, Castlefields

Daphne Mondon (5)	56
Daisy Ayris (5)	57
Ellouise Price (5)	58
Bella Jones (5)	59
Poppy Edwards (5)	60
Logan Moncrieff (4)	61
Rogan Matthews (5)	62
Grace Carroll (5)	63
Ivy Wildsmith (4)	64
Ollie Wilkinson (5)	65
Eddie Gaweda (5)	66

Montreal CE Primary School, Cleator Moor

Quinn Beeson (5)	67
Darcey Sharpe (5)	68
TJ Morgan (4)	69
Sophie Ritson (5)	70
Harry Cope (5)	71
Lucy Gearing (5)	72
Sophie-Grace Kelly (5)	73
Freddie Buchanan (4)	74

Smarden Primary School, Smarden

Freya Gibbs (5)	75
Ezra Wood (4)	76
Abdullah Refaie (5)	77
Mackie Allman (5)	78
Izzy Turner (5)	79
Mazie Bundy (4)	80
Bodhi Morris-Potter (5)	81
Chloe Tucker (5)	82

St Antony's RC Primary School, Woodford Green

Grayson Garr (5)	83
Eva Amodio (5)	84
Dominic Heneghan (5)	85
Jude Davies (4)	86
Christine Kostash (5)	87
Konstantin Woeste (5)	88

St Crispin's School, Leicester

Abbas Karim (5)	89
Tobias Atkin (5)	90
Jovan Gawera (5)	91
Joshua Muchira (4)	92
Lucas Nguyen (5)	93

St Martin's CE(VA) School, Epsom

Elias Rinks	94
Harry French (5)	95
George Ralls (5)	96
Isaac Stephens (5)	97
Sebastian Knowles (5)	98
Ollie Merchant (5)	99
Ava Hatchett-Cole (4)	100
Isaac Saul (5)	101
Max French (5)	102
Hannah Martin	103
Zané Brits	104
Alexa Gray (5)	105
Austin Walsh	106
Laurène Berry	107
Raffi Nott (4)	108
Johnny Gray (5)	109
Arson Tula (4)	110
Oscar Cox (5)	111
Aya Kirui (5)	112
Aeva Preedy-Leleu (5)	113
Emily Peacock (5)	114
Harvey Moss (5)	115
Maximus Coleman (5)	116
Jason Adeyemi	117

George Moorcraft (4)   118

St Mary's Catholic Primary School, Chesterfield

Minnie Garvey (5)	119
Mia Simpson (5)	120
Stefan Cox-Labo (5)	121
Colston Sutton (5)	122
Eve Hanson (5)	123
Freya Dixon (5)	124
Ornella Santoro (5)	125
Freya Williams (5)	126
Karolina Griniute (4)	127
Daniel Fearn (5)	128
Molly McGinley (5)	129
Arthur Jenkinson (5)	130
Thea Dias (5)	131
Bryony Read (5)	132
Cora Hendzell (4)	133

Vishnitz Girls' School, Hackney

Malka Seri Einhorn (6)	134
Chayelle Ackerman (6)	135
Chavi Bard (6)	136
Rivky Fruchter (6)	137
Bayla Schlesinger (6)	138
Suri Greenzweig (6)	139
Freidy Stockhamer (6)	140

Warley Road Academy, Halifax

Sharnelle Mawuwa (5)	141
Muhammad Umar Mahmood (5)	142
Noorayn Awan (5)	143
Salwa Noor (5)	144
Ismaeel Ramiz (4)	145
Subhan Hussain (4)	146
Jaylon Dearden (5)	147
Eesa Hussain (5)	148
Ayesha Shahzad (5)	149
Aizah Ateeq (5)	150
Ilyaana Butt (5)	151

Aizah Khan (5)	152
Ameliaa Akram (5)	153
Maya Rashid (5)	154
Hafsa Asad (5)	155
Maryam Khan (5)	156
Isaac Rauf (5)	157
Fatima Latif (5)	158

Wilberforce Primary School, Westminster

Teddy Collins (5)	159
Sienna Haliti (5)	160
Aseel Darwiche (4)	161
Amena Ahmed (4)	162
Taibah Khatun (5)	163
Adam Ahmed (5)	164
Ethan Flama (5)	165
Oscar Collins (5)	166
Shayan Rahman (5)	167
Rabab Ashmere (5)	168

THE RIDDLES

Catherine's First Riddle

What could it be?
Follow the clues and see.

It looks **like a big, white pillow**.
It sounds **like a washing machine**.
It smells **like carrots and grass**.
It feels **fluffy**.
It tastes **like chicken nuggets**.

Have you guessed what it could be?
Look below and you will see,
It is...

Answer: A horse.

Catherine Dusi (4)
Arksey Primary School, Arksey

Martha's First Riddle

What could it be?
Follow the clues and see.

It looks **as smooth as horses.**
It sounds **like a tiger's roar.**
It smells **like strawberries.**
It feels **soft.**
It tastes **like tomatoes and bread.**

Have you guessed what it could be?
Look below and you will see,
It is...

Answer: A polar bear.

Martha Rushbrooke (5)
Arksey Primary School, Arksey

Lucca's First Riddle

What could it be?
Follow the clues and see.

It looks **like it has a trunk like a pencil.**
It sounds **creaky like cracked wood.**
It smells **like wood.**
It feels **rough.**
It tastes **like a cracker.**

Have you guessed what it could be?
Look below and you will see,
It is...

Answer: An elephant.

Lucca White (5)
Arksey Primary School, Arksey

Oliver's First Riddle

What could it be?
Follow the clues and see.

It looks **like pencils**.
It sounds **like a mouse or a rat**.
It smells **like marshmallows**.
It feels **like cotton candy**.
It tastes **chilli and pepper**.

Have you guessed what it could be?
Look below and you will see,
It is...

Answer: A giraffe.

Oliver Gale (5)
Arksey Primary School, Arksey

Edie's First Riddle

What could it be?
Follow the clues and see.

It looks **like a chair**.
It sounds **like the rain**.
It smells **like a trump**.
It feels **like a wooden wall**.
It tastes **like a ham and cheese sandwich**.

Have you guessed what it could be?
Look below and you will see,
It is...

Answer: A zebra.

Edie Rollinson (5)
Arksey Primary School, Arksey

Harper's First Riddle

What could it be?
Follow the clues and see.

It looks **white and big**.
It sounds **like a lion**.
It smells **like pizza**.
It feels **like marshmallows**.
It tastes **like a barbecued T-bone**.

Have you guessed what it could be?
Look below and you will see,
It is...

Answer: A polar bear.

Harper Crundell (5)
Arksey Primary School, Arksey

Teodor's First Riddle

What could it be?
Follow the clues and see.

It looks **orange and black**.
It sounds **like a cat**.
It smells **like popcorn**.
It feels **soft and fluffy**.
It tastes **like a marshmallow**.

Have you guessed what it could be?
Look below and you will see,
It is...

Answer: A *tiger*.

Teodor Atkin (5)
Arksey Primary School, Arksey

Pippa's First Riddle

What could it be?
Follow the clues and see.

It looks **fluffy**.
It sounds **howly and loud**.
It smells **like cottage cheese**.
It feels **soft and warm**.
It tastes **like chocolate mints**.

Have you guessed what it could be?
Look below and you will see,
It is...

Answer: A wolf.

Pippa Jones (5)
Arksey Primary School, Arksey

Isaac's First Riddle

What could it be?
Follow the clues and see.

It looks **furry**.
It sounds **raah-ry**.
It smells **like rotten carrots**.
It feels **as fluffy as a kitten**.
It tastes **like beef noodles**.

Have you guessed what it could be?
Look below and you will see,
It is...

Answer: A *tiger*.

Isaac Lawrence (5)
Arksey Primary School, Arksey

Joseph's First Riddle

What could it be?
Follow the clues and see.

It looks **like a snake.**
It sounds **like a rattlesnake.**
It smells **like a red apple.**
It feels **soft.**
It tastes **like strawberries.**

Have you guessed what it could be?
Look below and you will see,
It is...

Answer: A tiger.

Joseph Carroll (5)
Arksey Primary School, Arksey

Daisy's First Riddle

What could it be?
Follow the clues and see.

It looks **orange and black**.
It sounds **like a monster**.
It smells **like strawberry laces**.
It feels **fluffy**.
It tastes **like meat**.

Have you guessed what it could be?
Look below and you will see,
It is...

Answer: A *tiger*.

Daisy Taylor (4)
Arksey Primary School, Arksey

Jessica's First Riddle

What could it be?
Follow the clues and see.

It looks **like ice**.
It sounds **like snow**.
It smells **like chocolate biscuits**.
It feels **like cucumber**.
It tastes **like cake**.

Have you guessed what it could be?
Look below and you will see,
It is...

Answer: *An elephant.*

Jessica Ellis (5)
Arksey Primary School, Arksey

Amelia's First Riddle

What could it be?
Follow the clues and see.

It looks **black and white**.
It sounds **like a horse**.
It smells **like chicken nuggets**.
It feels **fluffy**.
It tastes **like burgers**.

Have you guessed what it could be?
Look below and you will see,
It is...

Answer: A zebra.

Amelia Mangham (5)
Arksey Primary School, Arksey

Destiny's First Riddle

What could it be?
Follow the clues and see.

It looks **brown and big**.
It sounds **as loud as a police car**.
It smells **like cheese**.
It feels **soft**.
It tastes **like sauce**.

Have you guessed what it could be?
Look below and you will see,
It is...

Answer: An elephant.

Destiny Hockaday (5)
Arksey Primary School, Arksey

Jonathan's First Riddle

What could it be?
Follow the clues and see.

It looks **patchy**.
It sounds **like a baby snake**.
It smells **like chips**.
It feels **like cotton candy**.
It tastes **like apples**.

Have you guessed what it could be?
Look below and you will see,
It is...

Answer: A giraffe.

Jonathan Horberry
Arksey Primary School, Arksey

Brooke-Lilly's First Riddle

What could it be?
Follow the clues and see.

It looks **furry**.
It sounds **growly**.
It smells **like a potato**.
It feels **like marshmallows**.
It tastes **like sprouts**.

Have you guessed what it could be?
Look below and you will see,
It is...

Answer: A lion.

Brooke-Lilly Ackland (5)
Arksey Primary School, Arksey

Joshua's First Riddle

This is my riddle about a fantastic person.
Who could it be? Follow the clues to see!

This person has **black** hair,
Shorts are what they like to wear.
They like to watch **Sonic** on TV,
And play **Monopoly** with me.
They like **turkey** to eat,
And sometimes **cake** for a treat.
The computer is their favourite thing,
And **Friday** is what they sing.
Josh is their best friend,
And now this riddle is at the end.

Have you guessed who it could be?
Look below and you will see, it is...

Answer: Joe.

Joshua Thomson-Borg (11)
Bright Futures School, Lymm

Georgia's First Riddle

This is my riddle about an amazing animal.
What could it be?
Follow the clues to see!

This animal has **spikes** on its body,
And its colour is **green**.
This animal has **forest green** feet,
It likes **insects** to eat.
Underwater is where it lives,
Its favourite thing to do is **swim**.
This animal has **no** ears,
It makes **hissing** sounds for you to hear.

Are you an animal whizz?
Have you guessed what it is?
It is...

Answer: A crocodile.

Daphne Blake (Georgia) (6)
Bright Futures School, Lymm

Joshua's First Riddle

This is my riddle about an amazing animal.
What could it be?
Follow the clues to see!

This animal has **spots** on its body,
And its colour is **red**.
This animal has **no** feet,
It likes **leaves** to eat.
In the garden is where it lives,
Its favourite thing to do is **fly**.
This animal has **no** ears,
It makes **quiet** sounds for you to hear.

Are you an animal whizz?
Have you guessed what it is?
It is...

Answer: A ladybird.

Joshua Daniel Pierce (8)
Bright Futures School, Lymm

Ayrton's First Riddle

This is my riddle about an amazing animal.
What could it be?
Follow the clues to see!

This animal has **spots** on its body,
And its colour is **red**.
This animal has **black** feet,
It likes **leaves** to eat.
In the garden is where it lives.
This animal has **no** ears,
It makes **quiet** sounds for you to hear.

Are you an animal whizz?
Have you guessed what it is?
It is...

Answer: A ladybird.

Ayrton Ankrah (6)
Bright Futures School, Lymm

Archie's First Riddle

This is my riddle about a brilliant vehicle.
What could it be?
Follow the clues to see!

It has **six** wheels,
Fast is the speed it goes.
Its colour is **red**,
Two people can fit in it.
People use it to go to **fires**.

Have you guessed what it could be?
Look below and you will see,
It is...

Answer: A fire engine.

Archie Barrow (10)
Bright Futures School, Lymm

Freddie's First Riddle

What could it be?
Follow the clues and see.

It looks **small and orange**.
It sounds **quiet, it doesn't make a noise**.
It smells **horrible and stinky**.
It feels **wet and slippery**.
It tastes **fishy**.

Have you guessed what it could be?
Look below and you will see,
It is...

Answer: A *goldfish*.

Freddie Petrie (4)
Gawsworth Primary School, Gawsworth

Reuben's First Riddle

What could it be?
Follow the clues and see.

It looks **green, purple, black and white**.
It sounds **loud**.
It smells **nice and clean**.
It feels **hard**.
It tastes **like green paint**.

Have you guessed what it could be?
Look below and you will see,
It is...

Answer: *The Hulk.*

Reuben Cairns (5)
Gawsworth Primary School, Gawsworth

Amelie's First Riddle

What could it be?
Follow the clues and see.

It looks **shiny and red**.
It sounds **crunchy**.
It smells **spicy and makes me cough**.
It feels **smooth**.
It tastes **hot and fiery**.

Have you guessed what it could be?
Look below and you will see,
It is...

Answer: A chilli.

Amelie Carrier (5)
Gawsworth Primary School, Gawsworth

Hector's First Riddle

What could it be?
Follow the clues and see.

It looks **scary**.
It sounds **terrifying**.
It smells **woolly**.
It feels **furry**.
It tastes **like meat**.

Have you guessed what it could be?
Look below and you will see,
It is...

Answer: A smilodon.

Hector Stallard (5)
Gawsworth Primary School, Gawsworth

Alannah's First Riddle

What could it be?
Follow the clues and see.

It looks **like a witch's hair.**
It sounds **like the seaside.**
It smells **fishy.**
It feels **slimy.**
It tastes **salty.**

Have you guessed what it could be?
Look below and you will see,
It is...

Answer: Seaweed.

Alannah Corr (5)
Gawsworth Primary School, Gawsworth

Sam's First Riddle

What could it be?
Follow the clues and see.

It looks **messy**.
It sounds **like screaming**.
It smells **stinky**.
It feels **soft**.
It tastes **nice**.

Have you guessed what it could be?
Look below and you will see,
It is...

Answer: Baby Jack.

Sam Boyle (5)
Gawsworth Primary School, Gawsworth

Oscar's First Riddle

What could it be?
Follow the clues and see.

It looks **yellow**.
It sounds **crunchy**.
It smells **like seaweed**.
It feels **soft**.
It tastes **grainy**.

Have you guessed what it could be?
Look below and you will see,
It is...

Answer: *Sand.*

Oscar Smith (5)
Gawsworth Primary School, Gawsworth

Hermione's First Riddle

What could it be?
Follow the clues and see.

It looks **like a horse with a horn**.
It sounds **like neigh!**
It smells **like glitter**.
It feels **soft**.
It tastes **like hay**.

Have you guessed what it could be?
Look below and you will see,
It is...

Answer: A unicorn.

Hermione Woodley (4)
Grove CE Primary School, Grove

Bobby's First Riddle

What could it be?
Follow the clues and see.

It looks **like a jelly bean**.
It sounds **like snap!**
It smells **like water**.
It feels **spiky**.
It tastes **like meat**.

Have you guessed what it could be?
Look below and you will see,
It is...

Answer: A crocodile.

Bobby Saunders (5)
Grove CE Primary School, Grove

Maya's First Riddle

What could it be?
Follow the clues and see.

It looks **fluffy**.
It sounds **nibbly**.
It smells **fruity**.
It feels **furry**.
It tastes **like carrots**.

Have you guessed what it could be?
Look below and you will see,
It is...

Answer: A rabbit.

Maya Waring (5)
Grove CE Primary School, Grove

Brinley's First Riddle

What could it be?
Follow the clues and see.

It looks **pink**.
It sounds **like oink, oink!**
It smells **muddy**.
It feels **smooth**.
It tastes **like crunchy apples**.

Have you guessed what it could be?
Look below and you will see,
It is...

˙ƃıd ∀ :ɹǝʍsu∀

Brinley Bettson (5)
Grove CE Primary School, Grove

Darcey's First Riddle

What could it be?
Follow the clues and see.

It looks **cute**.
It sounds **loud**.
It smells **like dog treats**.
It feels **furry**.
It tastes **like dog bones**.

Have you guessed what it could be?
Look below and you will see,
It is...

Answer: A dog.

Darcey Austin (5)
Grove CE Primary School, Grove

George's First Riddle

What could it be?
Follow the clues and see.

It looks **fluffy**.
It sounds **like miaow!**
It smells **smelly**.
It feels **soft**.
It tastes **like cat food**.

Have you guessed what it could be?
Look below and you will see,
It is...

Answer: *A kitten.*

George Morgan (5)
Grove CE Primary School, Grove

Flyn's First Riddle

What could it be?
Follow the clues and see.

It looks **furry**.
It sounds **like miaow!**
It smells **like milk**.
It feels **soft**.
It tastes **like cat food**.

Have you guessed what it could be?
Look below and you will see,
It is...

Answer: A cat.

Flynn Bolton (4)
Grove CE Primary School, Grove

Henry's First Riddle

What could it be?
Follow the clues and see.

It looks **furry**.
It sounds **like neigh!**
It smells **like hay**.
It feels **soft**.
It tastes **like apples**.

Have you guessed what it could be?
Look below and you will see,
It is...

Answer: A horse.

Henry Addison (5)
Grove CE Primary School, Grove

Verity's First Riddle

What could it be?
Follow the clues and see.

It looks **muddy and pink**.
It sounds **like snort!**
It smells **muddy**.
It feels **smooth**.
It tastes **yucky**.

Have you guessed what it could be?
Look below and you will see,
It is...

Answer: A pig.

Verity Appleton (5)
Grove CE Primary School, Grove

Evie's First Riddle

What could it be?
Follow the clues and see.

It looks **white**.
It sounds **hoppy**.
It smells **stinky**.
It feels **fluffy**.
It tastes **like carrots**.

Have you guessed what it could be?
Look below and you will see,
It is...

Answer: A rabbit.

Evie Pryce (5)
Grove CE Primary School, Grove

Victoria's First Riddle

What could it be?
Follow the clues and see.

It looks **muddy**.
It sounds **like oink, oink!**
It smells **muddy**.
It feels **soft**.
It tastes **horrible**.

Have you guessed what it could be?
Look below and you will see,
It is...

Answer: A pig.

Victoria Jones (5)
Grove CE Primary School, Grove

George's First Riddle

What could it be?
Follow the clues and see.

It looks **fluffy**.
It sounds **like cluck!**
It smells **like egg**.
It feels **soft**.
It tastes **meaty**.

Have you guessed what it could be?
Look below and you will see,
It is...

Answer: A chicken.

George L. J. Vaughan (5)
Grove CE Primary School, Grove

Forest's First Riddle

What could it be?
Follow the clues and see.

It looks **grey**.
It sounds **like neigh!**
It smells **like hay**.
It feels **hairy**.
It tastes **like hay**.

Have you guessed what it could be?
Look below and you will see,
It is...

Answer: A horse.

Forest Slaymaker (5)
Grove CE Primary School, Grove

Noah's First Riddle

What could it be?
Follow the clues and see.

It looks **pink**.
It sounds **crunchy**.
It smells **like dirt**.
It feels **muddy**.
It tastes **like apples**.

Have you guessed what it could be?
Look below and you will see,
It is...

Answer: A pig.

Noah Arthur Alencar-Martins (5)
Grove CE Primary School, Grove

James' First Riddle

What could it be?
Follow the clues and see.

It looks **fluffy**.
It sounds **cute**.
It smells **like cat food**.
It feels **furry**.
It tastes **milky**.

Have you guessed what it could be?
Look below and you will see,
It is...

Answer: A kitten.

James Whyte (4)
Grove CE Primary School, Grove

Jacob's First Riddle

What could it be?
Follow the clues and see.

It looks **beautiful**.
It sounds **like miaow!**
It smells **hairy**.
It feels **soft**.
It tastes **yucky**.

Have you guessed what it could be?
Look below and you will see,
It is...

Answer: A cat.

Jacob Penn (5)
Grove CE Primary School, Grove

Halimah's First Riddle

This is my riddle about a fantastic person.
Who could it be? Follow the clues to see!

This person has **brown** hair,
Black shoes are what they like to wear.
They like to watch **the news** on TV,
And play **jigsaw puzzles** with me.
They like **fruit** to eat,
And sometimes **chocolate** for a treat.
Going to the shops is their favourite thing,
And **Twinkle, Twinkle, Little Star** is what they sing.
Halimah is their best friend,
And now this riddle is at the end.

Have you guessed who it could be?
Look below and you will see, it is...

Answer: My mum.

Halimah Sadia Shaffiq (4)
Lapage Primary School, Bradford

Hamda's First Riddle

This is my riddle about an amazing animal.
What could it be?
Follow the clues to see!

This animal has **spots** on its body,
And its colour is **orange**.
This animal has **four** feet,
It likes **animals** to eat.
Africa is where it lives,
Its favourite thing to do is **to run**.
This animal has **two** ears,
It makes **growling** sounds for you to hear.

Are you an animal whizz?
Have you guessed what it is?
It is...

Answer: A cheetah.

Hamda Sabir (5)
Lapage Primary School, Bradford

Hanna's First Riddle

This is my riddle about an amazing animal.
What could it be?
Follow the clues to see!

This animal has **wings** on its body,
And its colour is **brown**.
This animal has **two** feet,
It likes **insects and worms** to eat.
Its favourite thing to do is **fly**.
This animal has **no** ears,
It makes **tweet, tweet** sounds for you to hear.

Are you an animal whizz?
Have you guessed what it is?
It is...

Answer: A bird.

Hanna Butt
Lapage Primary School, Bradford

Yahya's First Riddle

This is my super first riddle.
What could it be?
Follow the clues to see!

In music is where you'll find it,
It's made out of **plastic**.
It is used for **making music**,
Its colour is **brown**.
It is a **circle** shape,
It has **a white top**.

Have you guessed what it could be?
Look below and you will see,
It is...

Answer: A drum.

Yahya Kalam (5)
Lapage Primary School, Bradford

Amani's First Riddle

This is my super first riddle.
What could it be?
Follow the clues to see!

In construction is where you'll find it,
It's made out of **wood**.
It is used for **playing**,
Its colour is **brown**.
It is a **circle** shape,
It has **four sides**.

Have you guessed what it could be?
Look below and you will see,
It is...

Answer: A block.

Amani (5)
Lapage Primary School, Bradford

Aaila's First Riddle

This is my super first riddle.
What could it be?
Follow the clues to see!

In music is where you'll find it,
It's made out of **plastic**.
It is used for **making music**,
Its colour is **black**.
It is a **circle** shape,
It has **balls**.

Have you guessed what it could be?
Look below and you will see,
It is...

Answer: A shaker.

Aaila (5)
Lapage Primary School, Bradford

Haseeb's First Riddle

This is my riddle about a brilliant vehicle.
What could it be?
Follow the clues to see!

It has **two** wheels,
Its colour is **black**,
One person can fit on it.
By riding it is how it moves,
People use it to go to **the park**.

Have you guessed what it could be?
Look below and you will see,
It is...

Answer: A bike.

Haseeb Mahmood (5)
Lapage Primary School, Bradford

Dua's First Riddle

This is my riddle about a brilliant vehicle.
What could it be?
Follow the clues to see!

It has **two wings**,
Fast is the speed it goes.
Its colour is **red**,
By flying is how it moves,
People use it to go to **Pakistan**.

Have you guessed what it could be?
Look below and you will see,
It is...

Answer: A jet.

Dua Khan (5)
Lapage Primary School, Bradford

Kiswa's First Riddle

What could it be?
Follow the clues and see.

It looks **like a ball**.
It sounds **juicy**.
It smells **sweet**.
It feels **hard**.
It tastes **sour**.

Have you guessed what it could be?
Look below and you will see,
It is...

Answer: An orange.

Kiswa Noor (5)
Lapage Primary School, Bradford

Khawlah's First Riddle

What could it be?
Follow the clues and see.

It looks **yellow**.
It sounds **soft**.
It smells **sweet**.
It feels **squidgy**.
It tastes **yummy**.

Have you guessed what it could be?
Look below and you will see,
It is...

Answer: A banana.

Khawlah Ayaz
Lapage Primary School, Bradford

Ajwa's First Riddle

What could it be?
Follow the clues and see.

It looks **round**.
It sounds **hard**.
It smells **sweet**.
It feels **cool**.
It tastes **yummy**.

Have you guessed what it could be?
Look below and you will see,
It is...

Answer: An apple.

Ajwa Nur (5)
Lapage Primary School, Bradford

Daphne's First Riddle

What could it be?
Follow the clues and see.

It looks **glittery and white**.
It sounds **like neighing**.
It smells **like flowers**.
It feels **silky**.
It tastes **like a candy cane**.

Have you guessed what it could be?
Look below and you will see,
It is...

Answer: A unicorn.

Daphne Mondon (5)
Martin Wilson School, Castlefields

Daisy's First Riddle

What could it be?
Follow the clues and see.

It looks **like a rainbow**.
It sounds **like a horse**.
It smells **like perfume**.
It feels **soft**.
It tastes **like flowers**.

Have you guessed what it could be?
Look below and you will see,
It is...

Answer: A unicorn.

Daisy Ayris (5)
Martin Wilson School, Castlefields

Ellouise's First Riddle

What could it be?
Follow the clues and see.

It looks **hairy**.
It sounds **like woof!**
It smells **like fleas**.
It feels **soft and cuddly**.
It tastes **like tinned food**.

Have you guessed what it could be?
Look below and you will see,
It is...

Answer: A dog.

Ellouise Price (5)
Martin Wilson School, Castlefields

Bella's First Riddle

What could it be?
Follow the clues and see.

It looks **gold and black**.
It sounds **cute**.
It smells **like flowers**.
It feels **furry**.
It tastes **like fish and mice**.

Have you guessed what it could be?
Look below and you will see,
It is...

Answer: A cat.

Bella Jones (5)
Martin Wilson School, Castlefields

Poppy's First Riddle

What could it be?
Follow the clues and see.

It looks **beautiful**.
It sounds **happy**.
It smells **lovely**.
It feels **soft**.
It tastes **like strawberries**.

Have you guessed what it could be?
Look below and you will see,
It is...

Answer: A unicorn.

Poppy Edwards (5)
Martin Wilson School, Castlefields

Logan's First Riddle

What could it be?
Follow the clues and see.

It looks **green**.
It sounds **munchy**.
It smells **like pears**.
It feels **hairy**.
It tastes **like plums**.

Have you guessed what it could be?
Look below and you will see,
It is...

Answer: A caterpillar.

Logan Moncrieff (4)
Martin Wilson School, Castlefields

Rogan's First Riddle

What could it be?
Follow the clues and see.

It looks **brown**.
It sounds **grizzly**.
It smells **like a forest**.
It feels **hairy**.
It tastes **like fish**.

Have you guessed what it could be?
Look below and you will see,
It is...

Answer: A bear.

Rogan Matthews (5)
Martin Wilson School, Castlefields

Grace's First Riddle

What could it be?
Follow the clues and see.

It looks **stripy**.
It sounds **scary**.
It smells **like a BBQ**.
It feels **angry**.
It tastes **like meat**.

Have you guessed what it could be?
Look below and you will see,
It is...

Answer: A tiger.

Grace Carroll (5)
Martin Wilson School, Castlefields

Ivy's First Riddle

What could it be?
Follow the clues and see.

It looks **fluffy**.
It sounds **loud**.
It smells **smoky**.
It feels **puffy**.
It tastes **like grass**.

Have you guessed what it could be?
Look below and you will see,
It is...

Answer: A sheep.

Ivy Wildsmith (4)
Martin Wilson School, Castlefields

Ollie's First Riddle

What could it be?
Follow the clues and see.

It looks **colourful**.
It sounds **cloppy**.
It smells **nice**.
It feels **soft**.
It tastes **hairy**.

Have you guessed what it could be?
Look below and you will see,
It is...

Answer: A unicorn.

Ollie Wilkinson (5)
Martin Wilson School, Castlefields

Eddie's First Riddle

What could it be?
Follow the clues and see.

It looks **big**.
It sounds **like ruff!**
It smells **muddy**.
It feels **excited**.
It tastes **yucky**.

Have you guessed what it could be?
Look below and you will see,
It is...

Answer: A dog.

Eddie Gaweda (5)
Martin Wilson School, Castlefields

Quinn's First Riddle

What could it be?
Follow the clues and see.

It looks **small and round**.
It sounds **squishy**.
It smells **sweet**.
It feels **soft**.
It tastes **delicious**.

Have you guessed what it could be?
Look below and you will see,
It is...

Answer: A blueberry.

Quinn Beeson (5)
Montreal CE Primary School, Cleator Moor

Darcey's First Riddle

What could it be?
Follow the clues and see.

It looks **like the moon**.
It sounds **quiet**.
It smells **like cream**.
It feels **soft**.
It tastes **nice**.

Have you guessed what it could be?
Look below and you will see,
It is...

Answer: A banana.

Darcey Sharpe (5)
Montreal CE Primary School, Cleator Moor

TJ's First Riddle

What could it be?
Follow the clues and see.

It looks **yellow**.
It sounds **like nothing**.
It smells **yummy**.
It feels **squishy**.
It tastes **sweet**.

Have you guessed what it could be?
Look below and you will see,
It is...

Answer: A banana.

TJ Morgan (4)
Montreal CE Primary School, Cleator Moor

Sophie's First Riddle

What could it be?
Follow the clues and see.

It looks **yellow**.
It sounds **squishy**.
It smells **like poop**.
It feels **squishy**.
It tastes **yummy**.

Have you guessed what it could be?
Look below and you will see,
It is...

Answer: A banana.

Sophie Ritson (5)
Montreal CE Primary School, Cleator Moor

Harry's First Riddle

What could it be?
Follow the clues and see.

It looks **like a ball**.
It sounds **crunchy**.
It smells **nice**.
It feels **hard**.
It tastes **good**.

Have you guessed what it could be?
Look below and you will see,
It is...

Answer: An apple.

Harry Cope (5)
Montreal CE Primary School, Cleator Moor

Lucy's First Riddle

What could it be?
Follow the clues and see.

It looks **round**.
It sounds **healthy**.
It smells **good**.
It feels **soft**.
It tastes **perfect**.

Have you guessed what it could be?
Look below and you will see,
It is...

Answer: An orange.

Lucy Gearing (5)
Montreal CE Primary School, Cleator Moor

Sophie-Grace's First Riddle

What could it be?
Follow the clues and see.

It looks **red**.
It sounds **quiet**.
It smells **nice**.
It feels **soft**.
It tastes **sweet**.

Have you guessed what it could be?
Look below and you will see,
It is...

Answer: A strawberry.

Sophie-Grace Kelly (5)
Montreal CE Primary School, Cleator Moor

Freddie's First Riddle

What could it be?
Follow the clues and see.

It looks **yellow**.
It sounds **quiet**.
It smells **yucky**.
It feels **soft**.
It tastes **nice**.

Have you guessed what it could be?
Look below and you will see,
It is...

Answer: A banana.

Freddie Buchanan (4)
Montreal CE Primary School, Cleator Moor

Freya's First Riddle

What could it be?
Follow the clues and see.

It looks **like no clouds**.
It sounds **like sunshine**.
It smells **like flowers**.
It feels **hot**.
It tastes **like sweets**.

Have you guessed what it could be?
Look below and you will see,
It is...

Answer: A sunny day.

Freya Gibbs (5)
Smarden Primary School, Smarden

Ezra's First Riddle

What could it be?
Follow the clues and see.

It looks **like little drops**.
It sounds **like pitter-patter!**
It smells **stinky**.
It feels **wet**.
It tastes **like water**.

Have you guessed what it could be?
Look below and you will see,
It is...

Answer: *Rain*.

Ezra Wood (4)
Smarden Primary School, Smarden

Abdullah's First Riddle

What could it be?
Follow the clues and see.

It looks **like a storm**.
It sounds **like pow!**
It smells **like danger**.
It feels **scary**.
It tastes **like ice**.

Have you guessed what it could be?
Look below and you will see,
It is...

Answer: Lightning.

Abdullah Refaie (5)
Smarden Primary School, Smarden

Mackie's First Riddle

What could it be?
Follow the clues and see.

It looks **like danger**.
It sounds **like thunder**.
It smells **salty**.
It feels **electric**.
It tastes **like water**.

Have you guessed what it could be?
Look below and you will see,
It is...

Answer: A storm.

Mackie Allman (5)
Smarden Primary School, Smarden

Izzy's First Riddle

What could it be?
Follow the clues and see.

It looks **colourful**.
It sounds **happy**.
It smells **like unicorns**.
It feels **magical**.
It tastes **sweet**.

Have you guessed what it could be?
Look below and you will see,
It is...

Answer: A rainbow.

Izzy Turner (5)
Smarden Primary School, Smarden

Mazie's First Riddle

What could it be?
Follow the clues and see.

It looks **white**.
It sounds **crunchy**.
It smells **like the rain**.
It feels **cold**.
It tastes **like a lolly**.

Have you guessed what it could be?
Look below and you will see,
It is...

Answer: *Snow.*

Mazie Bundy (4)
Smarden Primary School, Smarden

Bodhi's First Riddle

What could it be?
Follow the clues and see.

It looks **scary**.
It sounds **like bang!**
It smells **like danger**.
It feels **electric**.
It tastes **cold**.

Have you guessed what it could be?
Look below and you will see,
It is...

Answer: *Thunder.*

Bodhi Morris-Potter (5)
Smarden Primary School, Smarden

Chloe's First Riddle

What could it be?
Follow the clues and see.

It looks **white**.
It sounds **crunchy**.
It smells **like petals**.
It feels **fluffy**.
It tastes **like glitter**.

Have you guessed what it could be?
Look below and you will see,
It is...

Answer: Ice.

Chloe Tucker (5)
Smarden Primary School, Smarden

Grayson's First Riddle

What could it be?
Follow the clues and see.

It looks **red and shiny**.
It sounds **very loud and goes vroom!**
It smells **like burning**.
It feels **smooth and cold**.
It tastes **like nothing, you don't taste it**.

Have you guessed what it could be?
Look below and you will see,
It is...

Answer: A racing car.

Grayson Garr (5)
St Antony's RC Primary School, Woodford Green

Eva's First Riddle

What could it be?
Follow the clues and see.

It looks **long-necked**.
It sounds **like growling**.
It smells **like leaves**.
It feels **rough and scaly**.
It tastes **like plants**.

Have you guessed what it could be?
Look below and you will see,
It is...

Answer: A diplodocus.

Eva Amodio (5)
St Antony's RC Primary School, Woodford Green

Dominic's First Riddle

What could it be?
Follow the clues and see.

It looks **black and white**.
It sounds **screechy**.
It smells **really bad!**
It feels **furry**.
It tastes **good to Native Americans**.

Have you guessed what it could be?
Look below and you will see,
It is...

Answer: A skunk.

Dominic Heneghan (5)
St Antony's RC Primary School, Woodford Green

Jude's First Riddle

What could it be?
Follow the clues and see.

It looks **big and grey**.
It sounds **like brrrr!**
It smells **with its trunk**.
It feels **hard**.
It tastes **with its tongue**.

Have you guessed what it could be?
Look below and you will see,
It is…

Answer: An elephant.

Jude Davies (4)
St Antony's RC Primary School, Woodford Green

Christine's First Riddle

What could it be?
Follow the clues and see.

It looks **white**.
It sounds **squeaky**.
It smells **like grass**.
It feels **soft and fluffy**.
It tastes **like carrots**.

Have you guessed what it could be?
Look below and you will see,
It is...

Answer: A rabbit.

Christine Kostash (5)
St Antony's RC Primary School, Woodford Green

Konstantin's First Riddle

What could it be?
Follow the clues and see.

It looks **big**.
It sounds **scary**.
It smells **muddy**.
It feels **bumpy**.
It tastes **like meat**.

Have you guessed what it could be?
Look below and you will see,
It is...

Answer: A T-rex.

Konstantin Woeste (5)
St Antony's RC Primary School, Woodford Green

Abbas' First Riddle

What could it be?
Follow the clues and see.

It looks **red, blue, black and white**.
It sounds **whooshy**.
It smells **sweaty**.
It feels **smooth and hard**.
It tastes **like spiders' webs**.

Have you guessed what it could be?
Look below and you will see,
It is...

Answer: Spider-Man.

Abbas Karim (5)
St Crispin's School, Leicester

Tobias' First Riddle

What could it be?
Follow the clues and see.

It looks **rainbow coloured**.
It sounds **like squawk, squawk!**
It smells **like a jungle**.
It feels **soft and feathery**.
It tastes **super yucky**.

Have you guessed what it could be?
Look below and you will see,
It is...

Answer: A parrot.

Tobias Atkin (5)
St Crispin's School, Leicester

Jovan's First Riddle

What could it be?
Follow the clues and see.

It looks **like a square**.
It sounds **like clicking**.
It smells **like nothing**.
It feels **bumpy and flat**.
It tastes **cold**.

Have you guessed what it could be?
Look below and you will see,
It is...

Answer: Lego.

Jovan Gawera (5)
St Crispin's School, Leicester

Joshua's First Riddle

What could it be?
Follow the clues and see.

It looks **big and scary**.
It sounds **growly**.
It smells **dusty**.
It feels **hard and bumpy**.
It tastes **yucky**.

Have you guessed what it could be?
Look below and you will see,
It is...

Answer: A dinosaur.

Joshua Muchira (4)
St Crispin's School, Leicester

Lucas' First Riddle

What could it be?
Follow the clues and see.

It looks **scary and furry**.
It sounds **like roaring**.
It smells **stinky**.
It feels **soft**.
It tastes **dirty**.

Have you guessed what it could be?
Look below and you will see,
It is...

Answer: A lion.

Lucas Nguyen (5)
St Crispin's School, Leicester

Elias' First Riddle

What could it be?
Follow the clues and see.

It looks **like it has a mane**.
It sounds **like roar!**
It smells **like the clouds**.
It feels **warm**.
It tastes **like bunnies**.

Have you guessed what it could be?
Look below and you will see,
It is...

Answer: A lion.

Elias Rinks
St Martin's CE(VA) School, Epsom

Harry's First Riddle

What could it be?
Follow the clues and see.

It looks **like it has thick skin**.
It sounds **like stomping**.
It smells **fresh**.
It feels **smooth**.
It tastes **like plants**.

Have you guessed what it could be?
Look below and you will see,
It is...

Answer: A rhino.

Harry French (5)
St Martin's CE(VA) School, Epsom

George's First Riddle

What could it be?
Follow the clues and see.

It looks **like it has a mane**.
It sounds **like roar!**
It smells **like sausages**.
It feels **fluffy**.
It tastes **like humans**.

Have you guessed what it could be?
Look below and you will see,
It is...

Answer: A lion.

George Ralls (5)
St Martin's CE(VA) School, Epsom

Isaac's First Riddle

What could it be?
Follow the clues and see.

It looks **green**.
It sounds **scary**.
It smells **fiery**.
It feels **soft as it has feathers**.
It tastes **disgusting**.

Have you guessed what it could be?
Look below and you will see,
It is...

Answer: A dragon.

Isaac Stephens (5)
St Martin's CE(VA) School, Epsom

Sebastian's First Riddle

What could it be?
Follow the clues and see.

It looks **like it has black spots**.
It sounds **fast**.
It smells **fluffy**.
It feels **soft**.
It tastes **like meat**.

Have you guessed what it could be?
Look below and you will see,
It is...

Answer: A cheetah.

Sebastian Knowles (5)
St Martin's CE(VA) School, Epsom

Ollie's First Riddle

What could it be?
Follow the clues and see.

It looks **black and white**.
It sounds **squeaky**.
It smells **like fish**.
It feels **warm**.
It tastes **like fish**.

Have you guessed what it could be?
Look below and you will see,
It is...

Answer: A penguin.

Ollie Merchant (5)
St Martin's CE(VA) School, Epsom

Ava's First Riddle

What could it be?
Follow the clues and see.

It looks **like it has four legs**.
It sounds **like miaow!**
It smells **like meat**.
It feels **soft**.
It tastes **nice**.

Have you guessed what it could be?
Look below and you will see,
It is...

Answer: A cat.

Ava Hatchett-Cole (4)
St Martin's CE(VA) School, Epsom

Isaac's First Riddle

What could it be?
Follow the clues and see.

It looks **big and furry**.
It sounds **like roar!**
It smells **like fish**.
It feels **soft**.
It tastes **like a mouse**.

Have you guessed what it could be?
Look below and you will see,
It is...

Answer: A lion.

Isaac Saul (5)
St Martin's CE(VA) School, Epsom

Max's First Riddle

What could it be?
Follow the clues and see.

It looks **furry**.
It sounds **like twit-twoo!**
It smells **like mice**.
It feels **hungry**.
It tastes **like flies**.

Have you guessed what it could be?
Look below and you will see,
It is...

Answer: An owl.

Max French (5)
St Martin's CE(VA) School, Epsom

Hannah's First Riddle

What could it be?
Follow the clues and see.

It looks **orange**.
It sounds **like nothing**.
It smells **sweet**.
It feels **smooth**.
It tastes **like itself**.

Have you guessed what it could be?
Look below and you will see,
It is...

Answer: An orange.

Hannah Martin
St Martin's CE(VA) School, Epsom

Zané's First Riddle

What could it be?
Follow the clues and see.

It looks **pretty**.
It sounds **slow**.
It smells **like flowers**.
It feels **cuddly**.
It tastes **like make-up**.

Have you guessed what it could be?
Look below and you will see,
It is...

Answer: Rapunzel.

Zané Brits
St Martin's CE(VA) School, Epsom

Alexa's First Riddle

What could it be?
Follow the clues and see.

It looks **brown**.
It sounds **like oo, oo, aa, aa!**
It smells **fresh**.
It feels **soft**.
It tastes **dusty**.

Have you guessed what it could be?
Look below and you will see,
It is...

Answer: A monkey.

Alexa Gray (5)
St Martin's CE(VA) School, Epsom

Austin's First Riddle

What could it be?
Follow the clues and see.

It looks **stripy**.
It sounds **like roar!**
It smells **yucky**.
It feels **fluffy**.
It tastes **squishy**.

Have you guessed what it could be?
Look below and you will see,
It is...

Answer: A *tiger*.

Austin Walsh
St Martin's CE(VA) School, Epsom

Laurène's First Riddle

What could it be?
Follow the clues and see.

It looks **round**.
It sounds **crunchy**.
It smells **delicious**.
It feels **shiny**.
It tastes **fruity**.

Have you guessed what it could be?
Look below and you will see,
It is...

Answer: An apple.

Laurène Berry
St Martin's CE(VA) School, Epsom

Raffi's First Riddle

What could it be?
Follow the clues and see.

It looks **scary**.
It sounds **like roar!**
It smells **dirty**.
It feels **soft**.
It tastes **like meat**.

Have you guessed what it could be?
Look below and you will see,
It is...

Answer: A T-rex.

Raffi Nott (4)
St Martin's CE(VA) School, Epsom

Johnny's First Riddle

What could it be?
Follow the clues and see.

It looks **cute**.
It sounds **squeaky**.
It smells **lovely**.
It feels **nice**.
It tastes **disgusting**.

Have you guessed what it could be?
Look below and you will see,
It is...

Answer: A koala.

Johnny Gray (5)
St Martin's CE(VA) School, Epsom

Arson's First Riddle

What could it be?
Follow the clues and see.

It looks **green**.
It sounds **crunchy**.
It smells **very nice**.
It feels **smooth**.
It tastes **sweet**.

Have you guessed what it could be?
Look below and you will see,
It is...

Answer: A pear.

Arson Tula (4)
St Martin's CE(VA) School, Epsom

Oscar's First Riddle

What could it be?
Follow the clues and see.

It looks **round**.
It sounds **silent**.
It smells **nice**.
It feels **squishy**.
It tastes **sweet**.

Have you guessed what it could be?
Look below and you will see,
It is...

Answer: A blueberry.

Oscar Cox (5)
St Martin's CE(VA) School, Epsom

Aya's First Riddle

What could it be?
Follow the clues and see.

It looks **smooth**.
It sounds **like donk!**
It smells **fresh**.
It feels **smooth**.
It tastes **hard**.

Have you guessed what it could be?
Look below and you will see,
It is...

Answer: A stone.

Aya Kirui (5)
St Martin's CE(VA) School, Epsom

Aeva's First Riddle

What could it be?
Follow the clues and see.

It looks **yellow**.
It sounds **like splat!**
It smells **stinky**.
It feels **cold**.
It tastes **yummy**.

Have you guessed what it could be?
Look below and you will see,
It is...

Answer: Cheese.

Aeva Preedy-Leleu (5)
St Martin's CE(VA) School, Epsom

Emily's First Riddle

What could it be?
Follow the clues and see.

It looks **yellow**.
It sounds **quiet**.
It smells **fruity**.
It feels **squidgy**.
It tastes **yummy**.

Have you guessed what it could be?
Look below and you will see,
It is...

Answer: A banana.

Emily Peacock (5)
St Martin's CE(VA) School, Epsom

Harvey's First Riddle

What could it be?
Follow the clues and see.

It looks **round**.
It sounds **crunchy**.
It smells **sweet**.
It feels **smooth**.
It tastes **yummy**.

Have you guessed what it could be?
Look below and you will see,
It is...

Answer: An apple.

Harvey Moss (5)
St Martin's CE(VA) School, Epsom

Maximus' First Riddle

What could it be?
Follow the clues and see.

It looks **green**.
It sounds **crunchy**.
It smells **yummy**.
It feels **soft**.
It tastes **good**.

Have you guessed what it could be?
Look below and you will see,
It is...

Answer: Broccoli.

Maximus Coleman (5)
St Martin's CE(VA) School, Epsom

Jason's First Riddle

What could it be?
Follow the clues and see.

It looks **green**.
It sounds **soft**.
It smells **soft**.
It feels **smooth**.
It tastes **yummy**.

Have you guessed what it could be?
Look below and you will see,
It is...

Answer: A pear.

Jason Adeyemi
St Martin's CE(VA) School, Epsom

George's First Riddle

What could it be?
Follow the clues and see.

It looks **good**.
It sounds **quiet**.
It smells **nice**.
It feels **soft**.
It tastes **yummy**.

Have you guessed what it could be?
Look below and you will see,
It is...

Answer: Me!

George Moorcraft (4)
St Martin's CE(VA) School, Epsom

Minnie's First Riddle

This is my riddle about an amazing animal.
What could it be?
Follow the clues to see!

This animal has **wings** on its body,
And its colour is **like a rainbow**.
This animal has **four** feet,
It likes **glitter** to eat.
In the clouds is where it lives,
Its favourite thing to do is **fly**.
This animal has **two** ears,
It makes **magical** sounds for you to hear.

Are you an animal whizz?
Have you guessed what it is?
It is...

Answer: A unicorn.

Minnie Garvey (5)
St Mary's Catholic Primary School, Chesterfield

Mia's First Riddle

What could it be?
Follow the clues and see.

It looks **pretty and has four wings.**
It sounds **like fluttering.**
It smells **like pollen.**
It feels **soft and silky.**
It tastes **by using the taste sensors on its feet.**

Have you guessed what it could be?
Look below and you will see,
It is...

Answer: A butterfly.

Mia Simpson (5)
St Mary's Catholic Primary School, Chesterfield

Stefan's First Riddle

What could it be?
Follow the clues and see.

It looks **green like grass**.
It sounds **like a tired cricket**.
It smells **like muddy water**.
It feels **soft and squidgy like jelly**.
It tastes **like chicken**.

Have you guessed what it could be?
Look below and you will see,
It is...

Answer: A frog.

Stefan Cox-Labo (5)
St Mary's Catholic Primary School, Chesterfield

Colston's First Riddle

What could it be?
Follow the clues and see.

It looks **like a ball of fluff**.
It sounds **squeaky**.
It smells **like wood shavings**.
It feels **soft**.
It tastes **like carrots and broccoli**.

Have you guessed what it could be?
Look below and you will see,
It is...

Answer: A guinea pig.

Colston Sutton (5)
St Mary's Catholic Primary School, Chesterfield

Eve's First Riddle

What could it be?
Follow the clues and see.

It looks **like a cat**.
It sounds **like miaow!**
It smells **like a savannah**.
It feels **soft**.
It tastes **like kudu and hartebeest**.

Have you guessed what it could be?
Look below and you will see,
It is...

Answer: A cheetah.

Eve Hanson (5)
St Mary's Catholic Primary School, Chesterfield

Freya's First Riddle

What could it be?
Follow the clues and see.

It looks **like little clouds**.
It sounds **crunchy**.
It smells **like movie night**.
It feels **bumpy and hard**.
It tastes **yummy**.

Have you guessed what it could be?
Look below and you will see,
It is...

Answer: Popcorn.

Freya Dixon (5)
St Mary's Catholic Primary School, Chesterfield

Ornella's First Riddle

What could it be?
Follow the clues and see.

It looks **ginger and happy**.
It sounds **like it's purring**.
It smells **good**.
It feels **soft**.
It tastes **fishy**.

Have you guessed what it could be?
Look below and you will see,
It is...

Answer: A ginger cat.

Ornella Santoro (5)
St Mary's Catholic Primary School, Chesterfield

Freya's First Riddle

What could it be?
Follow the clues and see.

It looks **like two marshmallows**.
It sounds **quiet**.
It smells **like ice**.
It feels **cold**.
It tastes **refreshing**.

Have you guessed what it could be?
Look below and you will see,
It is...

Answer: A snowman.

Freya Williams (5)
St Mary's Catholic Primary School, Chesterfield

Karolina's First Riddle

What could it be?
Follow the clues and see.

It looks **grey and white**.
It sounds **like miaow!**
It smells **like fresh roses**.
It feels **fluffy**.
It tastes **furry**.

Have you guessed what it could be?
Look below and you will see,
It is...

Answer: A cat.

Karolina Griniute (4)
St Mary's Catholic Primary School, Chesterfield

Daniel's First Riddle

What could it be?
Follow the clues and see.

It looks **like water**.
It sounds **splishy splashy**.
It smells **fishy**.
It feels **wet and cold**.
It tastes **yucky**.

Have you guessed what it could be?
Look below and you will see,
It is...

Answer: *The ocean.*

Daniel Fearn (5)
St Mary's Catholic Primary School, Chesterfield

Molly's First Riddle

What could it be?
Follow the clues and see.

It looks **fluffy and cute**.
It sounds **like a duck**.
It smells **like fish**.
It feels **fluffy**.
It tastes **salty**.

Have you guessed what it could be?
Look below and you will see,
It is...

Answer: A penguin.

Molly McGinley (5)
St Mary's Catholic Primary School, Chesterfield

Arthur's First Riddle

What could it be?
Follow the clues and see.

It looks **big and strong**.
It sounds **loud and stompy**.
It smells **muddy**.
It feels **hard**.
It tastes **like grass**.

Have you guessed what it could be?
Look below and you will see,
It is...

Answer: A rhino.

Arthur Jenkinson (5)
St Mary's Catholic Primary School, Chesterfield

Thea's First Riddle

What could it be?
Follow the clues and see.

It looks **black and white**.
It sounds **like miaow!**
It smells **like fish**.
It feels **furry**.
It tastes **hairy**.

Have you guessed what it could be?
Look below and you will see,
It is...

Answer: A cat.

Thea Dias (5)
St Mary's Catholic Primary School, Chesterfield

Bryony's First Riddle

What could it be?
Follow the clues and see.

It looks **green**.
It sounds **like snap, snap!**
It smells **fishy**.
It feels **bumpy**.
It tastes **yucky**.

Have you guessed what it could be?
Look below and you will see,
It is...

Answer: A crocodile.

Bryony Read (5)
St Mary's Catholic Primary School, Chesterfield

Cora's First Riddle

What could it be?
Follow the clues and see.

It looks **tabby**.
It sounds **like purr!**
It smells **like a flower bed**.
It feels **soft**.
It tastes **milky**.

Have you guessed what it could be?
Look below and you will see,
It is...

Answer: A cat.

Cora Hendzell (4)
St Mary's Catholic Primary School, Chesterfield

Malka Seri's First Riddle

What could it be?
Follow the clues and see.

It looks **clear and bright**.
It sounds **like a bounce and a hop**.
It smells **sparkly and pure**.
It feels **fresh and cold**.
It tastes **like ice and water**.

Have you guessed what it could be?
Look below and you will see,
It is...

Answer: A raindrop.

Malka Seri Einhorn (6)
Vishnitz Girls' School, Hackney

Chayelle's First Riddle

What could it be?
Follow the clues and see.

It looks **like a rectangle**.
It sounds **like popping**.
It smells **like cocoa**.
It feels **hard and melted**.
It tastes **yummy and sweet**.

Have you guessed what it could be?
Look below and you will see,
It is...

Answer: Popping candy chocolate.

Chayelle Ackerman (6)
Vishnitz Girls' School, Hackney

Chavi's First Riddle

What could it be?
Follow the clues and see.

It looks **yellow and small**.
It sounds **chirpy**.
It smells **not very clean**.
It feels **cuddly and yummy**.
It tastes **like chicken**.

Have you guessed what it could be?
Look below and you will see,
It is...

Answer: A chick.

Chavi Bard (6)
Vishnitz Girls' School, Hackney

Rivky's First Riddle

What could it be?
Follow the clues and see.

It looks **round and tall**.
It sounds **like hissing**.
It smells **lemony and fresh**.
It feels **wet**.
It tastes **sharp**.

Have you guessed what it could be?
Look below and you will see,
It is...

Answer: A spray.

Rivky Fruchter (6)
Vishnitz Girls' School, Hackney

Bayla's First Riddle

What could it be?
Follow the clues and see.

It looks **soft and white**.
It sounds **like light hail**.
It smells **fresh**.
It feels **sandy**.
It tastes **salty**.

Have you guessed what it could be?
Look below and you will see,
It is...

Answer: Salt.

Bayla Schlesinger (6)
Vishnitz Girls' School, Hackney

Suri's First Riddle

What could it be?
Follow the clues and see.

It looks **gold**.
It sounds **like clanking**.
It smells **like metal**.
It feels **smooth**.
It tastes **hard**.

Have you guessed what it could be?
Look below and you will see,
It is...

Answer: A necklace.

Suri Greenzweig (6)
Vishnitz Girls' School, Hackney

Freidy's First Riddle

What could it be?
Follow the clues and see.

It looks **round**.
It sounds **delicious**.
It smells **yummy**.
It feels **sticky**.
It tastes **sweet**.

Have you guessed what it could be?
Look below and you will see,
It is...

Answer: A lolly.

Freidy Stockhamer (6)
Vishnitz Girls' School, Hackney

Sharnelle's First Riddle

What could it be?
Follow the clues and see.

It looks **like it has feathers**.
It sounds **like clucking**.
It smells **like food**.
It feels **soft**.
It tastes **disgusting**.

Have you guessed what it could be?
Look below and you will see,
It is...

Answer: A chicken.

Sharnelle Mawuwa (5)
Warley Road Academy, Halifax

Muhammad Umar's First Riddle

What could it be?
Follow the clues and see.

It looks **like it has feathers**.
It sounds **like buk, buk, buk!**
It smells **like poo**.
It feels **soft**.
It tastes **yummy**.

Have you guessed what it could be?
Look below and you will see,
It is...

Answer: A chicken.

Muhammad Umar Mahmood (5)
Warley Road Academy, Halifax

Noorayn's First Riddle

What could it be?
Follow the clues and see.

It looks **like it has feathers**.
It sounds **like cluck!**
It smells **like rubber**.
It feels **soft**.
It tastes **spicy**.

Have you guessed what it could be?
Look below and you will see,
It is...

Answer: A chicken.

Noorayn Awan (5)
Warley Road Academy, Halifax

Salwa's First Riddle

What could it be?
Follow the clues and see.

It looks **yellow**.
It sounds **like cock-a-doodle-doo!**
It smells **smelly**.
It feels **fluffy**.
It tastes **disgusting**.

Have you guessed what it could be?
Look below and you will see,
It is...

Answer: A chick.

Salwa Noor (5)
Warley Road Academy, Halifax

Ismaeel's First Riddle

What could it be?
Follow the clues and see.

It looks **like a bird**.
It sounds **like quack!**
It smells **like rubber**.
It feels **soft**.
It tastes **crunchy**.

Have you guessed what it could be?
Look below and you will see,
It is...

Answer: A duck.

Ismaeel Ramiz (4)
Warley Road Academy, Halifax

Subhan's First Riddle

What could it be?
Follow the clues and see.

It looks **fluffy**.
It sounds **like baa!**
It smells **fluffy**.
It feels **like a cloud**.
It tastes **like curry**.

Have you guessed what it could be?
Look below and you will see,
It is...

Answer: A sheep.

Subhan Hussain (4)
Warley Road Academy, Halifax

Jaylon's First Riddle

What could it be?
Follow the clues and see.

It looks **soft**.
It sounds **like baa!**
It smells **like wool**.
It feels **soft**.
It tastes **like chocolate**.

Have you guessed what it could be?
Look below and you will see,
It is...

Answer: A sheep.

Jaylon Dearden (5)
Warley Road Academy, Halifax

Eesa's First Riddle

What could it be?
Follow the clues and see.

It looks **wobbly**.
It sounds **like baa!**
It smells **grumpy**.
It feels **soft**.
It tastes **good**.

Have you guessed what it could be?
Look below and you will see,
It is...

Answer: A sheep.

Eesa Hussain (5)
Warley Road Academy, Halifax

Ayesha's First Riddle

What could it be?
Follow the clues and see.

It looks **black and white**.
It sounds **like moo!**
It smells **like poo**.
It feels **soft and dirty**.

Have you guessed what it could be?
Look below and you will see,
It is...

Answer: A cow.

Ayesha Shahzad (5)
Warley Road Academy, Halifax

Aizah's First Riddle

What could it be?
Follow the clues and see.

It looks **soft**.
It sounds **cute**.
It smells **like fish fingers**.
It feels **smooth**.

Have you guessed what it could be?
Look below and you will see,
It is...

Answer: A cat.

Aizah Ateeq (5)
Warley Road Academy, Halifax

Ilyaana's First Riddle

What could it be?
Follow the clues and see.

It looks **magical**.
It sounds **friendly**.
It smells **sweet**.
It feels **soft**.

Have you guessed what it could be?
Look below and you will see,
It is...

Answer: A unicorn.

Ilyaana Butt (5)
Warley Road Academy, Halifax

Aizah's First Riddle

What could it be?
Follow the clues and see.

It looks **fluffy**.
It sounds **grumpy**.
It smells **like grass**.
It feels **soft**.

Have you guessed what it could be?
Look below and you will see,
It is...

Answer: A sheep.

Aizah Khan (5)
Warley Road Academy, Halifax

Ameliaa's First Riddle

What could it be?
Follow the clues and see.

It looks **cute**.
It sounds **like miaow!**
It smells **like poo**.
It feels **fluffy**.

Have you guessed what it could be?
Look below and you will see,
It is...

Answer: A cat.

Ameliaa Akram (5)
Warley Road Academy, Halifax

Maya's First Riddle

What could it be?
Follow the clues and see.

It looks **fluffy**.
It sounds **like woof!**
It smells **like poo**.
It feels **wet**.

Have you guessed what it could be?
Look below and you will see,
It is...

Answer: A dog.

Maya Rashid (5)
Warley Road Academy, Halifax

Hafsa's First Riddle

What could it be?
Follow the clues and see.

It looks **woolly**.
It sounds **like baa!**
It smells **nice**.
It feels **soft**.

Have you guessed what it could be?
Look below and you will see,
It is...

Answer: A sheep.

Hafsa Asad (5)
Warley Road Academy, Halifax

Maryam's First Riddle

What could it be?
Follow the clues and see.

It looks **soft**.
It sounds **quiet**.
It smells **stinky**.
It feels **smooth**.

Have you guessed what it could be?
Look below and you will see,
It is...

Answer: A cat.

Maryam Khan (5)
Warley Road Academy, Halifax

Isaac's First Riddle

What could it be?
Follow the clues and see.

It looks **white**.
It sounds **funny**.
It smells **bad**.
It feels **furry**.

Have you guessed what it could be?
Look below and you will see,
It is...

Answer: A goat.

Isaac Rauf (5)
Warley Road Academy, Halifax

Fatima's First Riddle

What could it be?
Follow the clues and see.

It looks **soft**.
It sounds **loud**.
It smells **nice**.
It feels **grumpy**.

Have you guessed what it could be?
Look below and you will see,
It is...

Answer: A cat.

Fatima Latif (5)
Warley Road Academy, Halifax

Teddy's First Riddle

What could it be?
Follow the clues and see.

It looks **like it has a horn**.
It sounds **friendly**.
It smells **like candyfloss**.
It feels **like a rainbow**.
It tastes **like sweeties**.

Have you guessed what it could be?
Look below and you will see,
It is...

Answer: A unicorn.

Teddy Collins (5)
Wilberforce Primary School, Westminster

Sienna's First Riddle

What could it be?
Follow the clues and see.

It looks **like a white apple.**
It sounds **like a balloon.**
It smells **like cheese.**
It feels **like a rock.**
It tastes **not very nice.**

Have you guessed what it could be?
Look below and you will see,
It is...

Answer: The moon.

Sienna Haliti (5)
Wilberforce Primary School, Westminster

Aseel's First Riddle

What could it be?
Follow the clues and see.

It looks **like an aeroplane.**
It sounds **like a noisy blast-off.**
It smells **like fire.**
It feels **fast.**
It tastes **like space food.**

Have you guessed what it could be?
Look below and you will see,
It is...

Answer: A rocket.

Aseel Darwiche (4)
Wilberforce Primary School, Westminster

Amena's First Riddle

What could it be?
Follow the clues and see.

It looks **scary**.
It sounds **like a funny voice**.
It smells **like broccoli**.
It feels **like slime**.
It tastes **like cucumber**.

Have you guessed what it could be?
Look below and you will see,
It is...

Answer: An alien.

Amena Ahmed (4)
Wilberforce Primary School, Westminster

Taibah's First Riddle

What could it be?
Follow the clues and see.

It looks **like it has a ring**.
It sounds **like thunder**.
It smells **like gas**.
It feels **like air**.
It tastes **like candyfloss**.

Have you guessed what it could be?
Look below and you will see,
It is...

Answer: Saturn.

Taibah Khatun (5)
Wilberforce Primary School, Westminster

Adam's First Riddle

What could it be?
Follow the clues and see.

It looks **like a red ball**.
It sounds **like cars**.
It smells **like fire**.
It feels **hot**.
It tastes **like a chocolate bar**.

Have you guessed what it could be?
Look below and you will see,
It is...

Answer: Mars.

Adam Ahmed (5)
Wilberforce Primary School, Westminster

Ethan's First Riddle

What could it be?
Follow the clues and see.

It looks **round and white**.
It sounds **crumbly**.
It smells **like cheese**.
It feels **like sand**.
It tastes **crunchy**.

Have you guessed what it could be?
Look below and you will see,
It is...

Answer: The moon.

Ethan Flama (5)
Wilberforce Primary School, Westminster

Oscar's First Riddle

What could it be?
Follow the clues and see.

It looks **fluffy**.
It sounds **like miaow!**
It smells **like a unicorn**.
It feels **soft**.
It tastes **like cat food**.

Have you guessed what it could be?
Look below and you will see,
It is...

Answer: A cat.

Oscar Collins (5)
Wilberforce Primary School, Westminster

Shayan's First Riddle

What could it be?
Follow the clues and see.

It looks **red**.
It sounds **like a spaceship**.
It smells **like chocolate**.
It feels **hot**.
It tastes **like space**.

Have you guessed what it could be?
Look below and you will see,
It is...

Answer: Mars.

Shayan Rahman (5)
Wilberforce Primary School, Westminster

Rabab's First Riddle

What could it be?
Follow the clues and see.

It looks **yellow**.
It sounds **like fun**.
It smells **like dirt**.
It feels **hot**.
It tastes **like hot rice**.

Have you guessed what it could be?
Look below and you will see,
It is...

Answer: The sun.

Rabab Ashmere (5)
Wilberforce Primary School, Westminster

YoungWriters Est. 1991

YOUNG WRITERS INFORMATION

We hope you have enjoyed reading this book – and that you will continue to in the coming years.

If you're the parent or family member of an enthusiastic poet or story writer, do visit **www.youngwriters.co.uk/subscribe** and sign up to receive news, competitions, writing challenges and tips, activities and much, much more! There's lots to keep budding writers motivated!

If you would like to order further copies of this book, or any of our other titles, then please give us a call or order via your online account.

Young Writers
Remus House
Coltsfoot Drive
Peterborough
PE2 9BF
(01733) 890066
info@youngwriters.co.uk

Join in the conversation!
Tips, news, giveaways and much more!

YoungWritersUK YoungWritersCW youngwriterscw